Walter Scott dra[...] [...]y.
1814 Year of Wa[...] [...] through
Scott's life and ex[...] [...]g umes expanding from
his career in Edinburgh and the Borders, as
invalid, schoolboy, lawyer, translator, his first
successes as a ballad-collector and poet –
backgrounded by the French and industrial
revolutions.

People today still get hooked on Walter Scott,
and e-readers can present his world in large
instead of miniscule type. It all really took off
with the 'sensation' of *Waverley*, or *'Tis Sixty
Years Since*, set in the Jacobite rebellion of
1745.

With Scoular Anderson's cartoons and the magic
of QR access to virtual Scott-land on the
internet, see how the scenes and dilemmas of
Scott's characters still matter today!

Clan Scotland series

also in this series
Scotland the Brief
a short history of a nation

1814 YEAR OF
WAVERLEY

HOW WALTER SCOTT'S NOVEL
CHANGED US

CHRISTOPHER HARVIE

cheerfully illustrated
by Scoular Anderson

ARGYLL ✤ PUBLISHING

© Christopher Harvie 2013

Argyll Publishing
Glendaruel
Argyll PA22 3AE
Scotland
www.argyllpublishing.co.uk

The author has asserted
his moral rights.

**British Library
Cataloguing-in-
Publication Data.
A catalogue record for
this book is available
from the British Library.**

ISBN 978 1 908931 23 8

Printing:
Martins the Printers,
Berwick-upon-Tweed

This book is in memory of my parents' friends Barbara Wood and Robbie Robertson, East Avenel, Melrose. Better neighbours they could not have had. Their ashes lie strewn at Scott's View, Bemersyde, where they'd drive to admire the Eildons at evening, and eat fish and chips.

Contents

Preface

TO EXAMINE Walter Scott's novel *Waverley* along with the books and careers that prefaced and followed it, is to sense its vitality. 'It shows how many ways there are of being alive,' albeit sometimes involving screeching gear-changes from one chapter to another, and across several energetic lives.

Man and books may be in for a revival. Although Scott can be long-winded, his small-type pages can now be magnified by the e-reader.

Waverley contains 'pictures and conversations', travel, money, love, scenery, drinking, hunting, imprisonment, royalty, religious mania, music, battles, food, costumes, strange languages and horror. Somehow, at the end, young Edward Waverley makes sense of this and settles down. . . and Sir Walter was for eighteen turbulent years after 1814 to bestride Scotland as Napoleon earlier bestrode France.

This is the second book in the 'Clan Scotland'

series. I want to thank Alice Lowenstein, Christine Frasch, Sue Bennett, Douglas Lowndes, Allan Massie, Derek Rodger and Caroline McCracken-Flesher. All have tolerated and juggled with the ideas and opinions of this book, which is, like Scott's *Waverley* itself, experimental.

If this book seems closer to modern life and the treasure-house of the internet than the sharp-eyed but sheltered order of contemporary authors like Jane Austen, part of it is due to Walter Scott himself.

Waverley is place, person and character: open and undecided. Random facts and people are thrown together into a novel which, like a machine, gives a pattern. The kaleidoscope was also invented in Scotland in 1814 by Scott's Melrose friend the optical scientist Sir David Brewster (1781-1868). *Waverley* remains, I hope, *there*, mapped but unprécised: like the Eildon Hills or Ben Ledi rising from the mists, for you to read.

The approach of my text is also different. It's a dialogue with material you can either buy very cheaply for an e-reader or download on your computer. It's not intended to repeat info and ideas you get from the texts, but to get you to ask questions of these texts and of your own knowledge.

At the Open University, founded 1969, I was one of the first historians. Our inspirations were radical historians and critics like E. P. Thompson or Raymond Williams who were in touch with the culture from which the industrial labour movement sprang, in the middle years of Walter Scott's life. Central to this was John Bunyan's *The Pilgrim's Progress*, a 'road-movie'-type story with Bible texts, found in every cottar's home. Although no longer orthodox Christians (and Scott himself was non-religious as well as Conservative) they were active political radicals. They could understand this sort of appeal, and the importance within it of dialogue: not telling but learning. Which is roughly how this book, as well as *Waverley*, proceeds.

Christopher Harvie
Avenel, Melrose
20 February 2013

PART I
MAN, POET, NOVELIST

'Walter Scott has no business to write novels, especially good ones. He has Fame and Profit enough as a Poet. I do not like him, and do not mean to like *Waverley* if I can help it – but fear I must.'

Jane Austen, 1814

Entertaining Miss Austen
'The big Bow-Wow strain I can do myself
like any now going; but the exquisite touch
which renders ordinary commonplace things and
characters interesting is denied to me.'

1. Scott the Man

FOCUS FIRST ON Scott the man. A frail, polio-crippled boy turned solid conservative lawyer and fashionable narrative poet by 1814. He had been born in Edinburgh in 1771 into the picturesque and varied society that crowded the Old Town on its volcanic spine between Castle and Holyrood Palace. Its four-to-ten storey 'lands' had genteel drawing rooms on their middle floors, tradesmen below, howffs (pubs) next the closes, servants and the poor in the attics and cellars.

Slums were everywhere, human sewage slurped through the streets. The Scotts lost seven out of twelve children to early death. Walter survived by being sent to the Borders: 'Old unhappy far-off things and battles long ago.' Central to the experience of the young Scott was the fact that most lives were short and memory mattered.

An imaginative writer and historian, he could use his family's own part in the events *Waverley*

New technology has already revived twenty-first
century Scott. You can get hold of all sorts of
out-of-copyright material by Scott and his

described; which Scott recorded, organised, illustrated and publicised.

Scott was historian, dramatist, folklorist, poet,
song collector, novelist, editor: awesomely productive
in only sixty one years, first as a ballad collector,
then a narrative poet with *The Lay of the Last
Minstrel* in 1805. In 1810, his *The Lady of the Lake*
arguably helped to create the modern Scots tourist
industry. After *Waverley* came out, with Scott's
authorship an open secret, he managed a remarkable
average of two full-length novels a year and ran his
own publishing company. He built up a world-
reference system, but was also rooted in his Borders
as Sheriff of Selkirk, first at Ashiestiel (close to
Traquair, a model for *Waverley's* 'Tully-Veolan') then
at Abbotsford, built 1814-25.

You can treat the story of Scott and *Waverley* as
landscape and swim around within this largely
Scottish-inspired tradition. Once you get into the
books of Scott you'll find that his style and characters
make up a huge and complex world. Baron Bradwardine can ramble and Scott indulges him, but you
can end up fond of the old man, tolerating his defeat
and poverty, as long as he has his beloved Livy (the
historian of the Roman republic) to read.

contemporaries online, and the Waverley novels are widely available online as downloads for e-readers – often completely free!

Scott can also be sharp. Think of his Edinburgh folk in *The Heart of Midlothian* regretting the loss of their Parliament in 1707: 'We could aye peeble them when they waurna gude bairns, but naebody's claws can reach the length o' Lunnon.'

He can be naughty. The introduction to *The Lady of the Lake* has James Hogg describing the popularity of King James V of Scotland (1513-42) through a 'somewhat licentious' old ballad:

> He took a bugle frae his side,
> He blew both wide and shrill,
> And four-and-twenty belted knights
> Came skipping o'er the hill.
> Then he took out a little knife,
> 'Let all his duddies fa', [breeches]
> And he was the brawest gentleman
> That was amang them aa.

And he can pity the vulnerable – the brave and truly pathetic, like poor Lucy Ashton in *The Bride of Lammermoor*: a girl who wants love and will never find it, whom war and family conflict will drive mad:

> Look not thou on beauty's charming,
> Sit thou still when kings are arming,
> Taste not when the wine-cup glistens,

Speak not when the people listens,
Stop thine ear against the singer,
From the red gold keep thy finger;
Vacant heart and hand and eye,
Easy live and quiet die.

If this sounds Shakespearian, it is. It doesn't imitate but shows Scott had the same sort of imagination: the vast curiosity and learning coupled with the poetic and emotional effect that D.H. Lawrence once demonstrated, grabbing his stomach, 'to hit you *there!*'

The core *Waverley* novels deal with Scottish history between the Reformation of 1560 and the aftermath of the Napoleonic Wars. But Scott was also business-minded, saw what paid, and applied his Scots style to the English middle ages with *Ivanhoe* (1819), the most successful of all his books, printing three times the editions of *Waverley*.

The Talisman (1825) took on the Crusades from a critical point-of-view, sympathetic to Islam. He also shrewdly analysed the making of 'Great Britain'.

Kenilworth (1821) on the intrigues around Queen Elizabeth, was followed by *The Fortunes of Nigel* (1822) on her successor James Stewart, the Sixth and First, entering in 1603 on his London inheritance. 'From today, for the King, every day will be Christmas.'

The slump of 1825 landed Scott with the modern equivalent of £20 million in debt. In his last years at his 'fiction factory', the baronial villa of Abbotsford 35 miles south of Edinburgh in the Tweed valley, he became his own subject, writing *The Life of Napoleon*, really a contemporary history of Europe, his testamentary *Journal*, and the bleak Canongate stories.

He researched a complex documentation of his own work in the definitive 'magnum opus' (*The Lady of the Lake* alone acquired 140 pages of footnotes!) until his health collapsed. A Mediterranean trip on a British warship didn't help. After completing a spectral Grand Tour he returned by steamboat and coach from Leith to die at home on 21 September 1832.

Young Wattie at Smailholm Tower
Breathes there the man with soul so dead,
That never to himself hath said,
This is my own, my native land!

2. Scott in Company

SCOTT WASN'T alone. He was one of a very articulate group of Scots poets, fictionalists, critics and reviewers, writing in the early 1800s in a variety of styles, who included (or sometimes didn't include – falling-outs were frequent):

James Hogg 'the Ettrick Shepherd' (1770-1835) poet, storyteller and folklore collector, parodist, author of an extraordinary psychological novel *The Memoirs and Confessions of a Justified Sinner* (1822).

John Galt (1779-1839), political agent, early imperialist, satirist of Scottish politics in *Annals of the Parish* and *The Provost* (1821-22).

John Leyden (1775-1811), poet, clergyman, lawyer, folklorist, multitalent, imperialist and linguist.

Susan Ferrier (1782-1854) 'full of humour and ready with repartee', friend and a robust sort of northern Jane Austen in *Marriage* (1818).

If you lived in 1814, what would your life be like? What job would you do? How healthy, wealthy or educated would you be? How much influence and

Sir Henry Raeburn (1756-1823) and **Sir David Wilkie** (1785-1841), painters of Scots grandees and ordinary folk going about their lives.

George Gordon, Lord Byron (1788-1824), great lover, satirist, Greek patriot. . .

. . . and maybe also **Edgar Allan Poe** (1809-1849) who was in Irvine, Scotland, in 1815 as a very precocious wee boy. Where would Hollywood horror or Hammer Films, let alone the crime story, have been without him?

. . . and **Mary Godwin** (1797-1851) daughter of the feminist Mary Wollstonecraft and the 'Jacobin' novelist William Godwin, came north as the friend of the Baxter family in Dundee. She would, along with her husband, the poet Shelley and Byron animate *Frankenstein* in 1819.

. . . and **Thomas Carlyle** (1795-1881) social critic, experimental novelist, Victorian 'sage' who exports this activity to London, eloquently assaults industrialisation and *laissez-faire*, influences Charles Dickens, John Ruskin, Karl Marx and Walt Whitman.

So on Scott's fringes lie the Gothic tale, the Who-

power would you have over your own life, issues affecting your family, society, or the world around you?

dunit, the Bug-Eyed Monster of Science Fiction, revolutionary socialism.

Was there something in the water in Scotland at this time that encouraged such expression? What kind of society was handed down from previous generations? Was it Scots education that enabled individual writers and thinkers to link to a society in which both philosophy and psychology were valued?

One innovation Walter Scott championed – which saved a lot of people a lot of time – was the political/literary review. The *Edinburgh Review* (1802) or *Blackwood's Magazine* (1817) meant that you could get the gist of a book from an anonymous 'notice' without having to plough through. Edinburgh was the birthplace of *Encyclopaedia Britannica* (founded there, 1769) and atlases, and gazetteers, and 'academic editions' of classics.

Edinburgh locals would argue that this was also enabled by the existence of a big papermaking industry in the water-powered mills of the towns to the south, and mechanical engineering which built and maintained modern presses, bookbinding machines and block-making devices.

The year 2014 is jam-packed with anniversaries for Scots. Two hundred years since the publication of *Waverley*. Can you think of any others?

You're probably already familiar with Jane Austen's polite horse-drawn world, wandered wild in the Brontes' Yorkshire and thrown yourself into the adventures of C.S. Forester's *Hornblower* or Patrick O'Brian's *Jack Aubrey* novels. You may have been captured by Thackeray's *Vanity Fair* (1848) fascinated and appalled by the minx Becky Sharp intriguing among the political elite, or plunged into Tolstoy's *War and Peace* (1865-9), fallen in love with Natasha, trudged with Pierre through the horrors of the Russian winter of 1812.

And Scotland? You've probably read some Robert Burns (1759-96), and gone with him to the howffs (pubs) and across the ploughlands of Kyle in Ayrshire, or heard and smelt the rattle and fug of the new cotton factories if you've visited New Lanark, or seen the displays in the Edinburgh Portrait Gallery and National Museum. You will have heard the Clearances – evictions from the glens – talked about, particularly if you bear a Highland name. Or have scrambled with David Balfour and Alan Breck through the Highlands after the Forty-Five in R.L. Stevenson's *Kidnapped* (1886).

1814 came at the end of a near-unbroken war between Britain and France that started in 1793.

---

e.g. 1314 Battle of Bannockburn, 1714 death of Queen Anne, 1814 Congress of Vienna, 1914 Outbreak of World War I.

Walter Scott came to maturity at the end of an active century. His mentor Adam Ferguson collected and systematised prevailing ideas in his *History of Civil Society* (1767) as a central figure in what was later called the 'Scottish Enlightenment' – meaning the contributions of William Robertson, David Hume, Thomas Reid and Adam Smith to philosophy, science, literature and social studies.

Ferguson saw commerce taking over from conflict, yet it was only in 1814 that Europe and the USA drew breath from four decades of fighting: both high-minded and quite bloody. Revolutionary then Napoleonic France had overrun the European land-mass, from Lisbon to Moscow. Napoleon rationalised it in 1806 into a structure of national monarchies, often run by his family, pushing aside the old ramshackle international orders of the Austrian empire and the Papacy.

Happy hours with Mistress Hogg, Liddesdale
'He pierced him through and through the heart,
He mauled him cruelly;
Then hung him ower the draw-brig
Beside the ither three.'

3. Folklorist into Poet

WHY SHOULD YOU be interested in Scott's poetry? We seem to encounter Burns everywhere, but Scott, once wildly popular, seems as dead as a leg of Border mutton. Wrong.

Look into *The Lady of the Lake* and *Marmion* (1808) and you'll find that they rattle along. The shorter lyrics that stud them are often gems. As an introduction, read 'Young Lochinvar' (you will find it in Canto XX in *Marmion*). Try reading it out loud.

O young Lochinvar is come out of the west,
Through all the wide Border his steed was the best;
And save his good broadsword he weapons had
                                                                    none,
He rode all unarm'd, and he rode all alone.
So faithful in love, and so dauntless in war,
There never was knight like the young Lochinvar.
. . .
There was mounting 'mong Graemes of the
                                                        Netherby clan;
Forsters, Fenwicks, and Musgraves, they rode and
                                                        they ran:

There was racing and chasing on Canobie Lee,
But the lost bride of Netherby ne'er did they see.
So daring in love, and so dauntless in war,
Have ye e'er heard of gallant like young Lochinvar?

It's a great adventure, with all the ingredients of romance – 'boy meets girl, boy loses girl, boy gets girl' – and the metre Scott uses means that it gallops along on all four legs. Scott's challenge is not to get dragged away by this. So he inserts calmer passages, *'Love swells like the Solway, but ebbs like its tide'* and lighter conversations, like those of Ellen's bridesmaids.

The poem has a precise geography and background politics. The Solway is the Border Firth: Canonbie and Netherby are Border settlements, north and south of the Esk, which feeds it. Netherby was the castle of the English branch of the Grahams/ Graemes, a clan found on both sides, though being close neighbours had little to do with friendship. Take the name 'Lochinvar': not border but Gaelic, though Galloway Gaelic. So there's an element here of national antagonism.

Ellen is being married to a nasty piece-of-work, 'a laggard in love and a coward in war,' for diplomatic reasons. So Lochinvar makes off with her – just as the virile Romans stole the Sabine girls. In fact Scott's symbolism was pretty explicit, *'and the groom was left dangling his bonnet and plume,'* says it all.

All this is pretty nationalistic and socially healthy. Families renewed themselves by *'exogamy'* (taking brides from rival tribes) and this becomes even more the case when we look at who's singing the story in *Marmion*. Lady Heron is King James IV's mistress, showing a lot of pretty bosom, promising more fun (the king had many 'natural' children) and the rascally Lord Marmion is up for this as well.

It's also the eve of war with England in 1513, so the mix of sex and violence goes down well at the Scots Court in Linlithgow. Though the outcome will be tragic: not far south of another Border river, the Tweed, catastrophe waited at Flodden field.

This reflects Scott's own knowledge of his country's literature, the background to *The Minstrelsy of the Scottish Border* (1802). He followed *Ossian* (1761-62) written by its 'discoverer' James MacPherson, but an oral culture certainly existed and the controversy over it echoed throughout Europe.

In 1802, collecting poems in Liddesdale, Scott first met Hogg, 'the Ettrick Shepherd' and his mother, who sang them the old ballads reluctantly:

> 'There was never ane o' my sangs prentit till ye prentit them yoursel. . . They were made for singin' an' no for readin' but ye have broken the charm now, and they'll never be sung mair.'

Why were the ballads important? They had to rhyme, because this helped memorising them: once you have memorised a poem, you won't forget it. For people living in remote places, without clocks and with sundials unreliable – this is Scotland! – notable events such as floods, battles, snowstorms, sudden deaths – were means of marking time, just as earlier peoples had used stone circles to mark the movements of the sun. Only in the late 1600s (when clocks appeared – Scotland's oldest is at Douglas Kirk, 1650) did literacy make a real impact. This was a two-edged weapon, much of the print being devoted to religion.

Scott's first ballads were trial efforts and he knew they were. But he combined the form with the fireworks of the court poets. These have complex rhyme-schemes, choruses, 'conceits' (clever tricks, parodies) and rich descriptions, which he could match, and slot in footnotes that discuss references and events. Cosmo Comyn Bradwardine is himself a sort of living footnote!

Scott's narrative poems were set in medieval Scotland, and in understanding the period, archives were important. But those of the Scots crown were sent south by Oliver Cromwell in 1650, when he invaded. Charles II sent them back by two ships, one of which was lost.

A limited amount of printed material, local chronicles and family records accumulated in Register House in 1780s Edinburgh, and thankfully ballad-style narratives, such as Archdeacon Barbour's 'The Brus' (1378) and Blind Harry's partisan 'The Wallace' (1480) survived.

Scott consciously supplemented these with: *The Lay of the Last Minstrel* (Douglas and Scott politics c.1400), *Marmion* (Flodden, 1513), *The Lord of the Isles* (Bruce's Campaign, 1308-14) and *The Lady of the Lake* (the reign of James V, c. 1530).

They were, in a way, tributes to the great years of Scottish poetry, during a period when England's expulsion from France and the War of the Roses dried

Robert Burns is one of the most popular Scottish poets ever. How many of his poems do you know? Can you recite any from memory? Can you sing any of his songs?

up the poetic flow of the likes of Geoffrey Chaucer. The age of William Dunbar, Robert Henryson, Bishop Gavin Douglas, who translated Virgil's *Aeneid* into Scots, was mourned by the Jacobite publisher Allan Ramsay:

> Our country then a tale cou'd tell,
> Europe had nane mair snack and snell
> At verse and prose.
> Our kings were poets too themsell,
> Bauld and jocose.

4. Poet into Novelist

IN 1812, the following hit British publishing.

Ye who shall marvel when you hear her tale,
Oh! had you known her in her softer hour,
Mark'd her black eye that mocks her coal-
                              black veil,
Heard her light, lively tones in Lady's bower,
Seen her long locks that foil the painter's
                              power,
Her fairy form, with more than female grace,
Scarce would you deem that Saragoza's tower
Beheld her smile in Danger's Gorgon face,
Thin the closed ranks, and lead in Glory's
                              fearful chase.

This is from the first Canto of *Childe Harold's Pilgrimage* by George Gordon, Lord Byron. 'Born half a Scot and bred a whole one' he burst onto the literary market in 1809. A friend of Shelley and Keats, revolutionary, libertine, intimate eroticist, Byron commemorated the Spanish-British expulsion of the French from Spain – Europe was open again! He

Competition!
'I see their glorious black eyes shine
But gazing on each glowing maid,
My own the burning tear-drop laves,
To think such breasts should suckle slaves!'
'Oooooh!'

stretched the bounds of permissiveness in poetry while at the same time appealing to a serious, sin-conscious generation.

In comparison, Scott seemed on the dry side. He was stretched for cash, and seems to have refocused his energy on a Border lawman, historian, publisher life. New options were obviously opening as after 1812, Napoleon was in retreat and a line was drawn under the excitements of nearly twenty years of near-total war. If poetry was to be sensationalist and escapist, Byron could do it better.

In 1807, Scott had contributed the final chapter to an unfinished manuscript, *Queen-Hoo Hall* by Joseph Strutt, who had died before it could be completed. This started him thinking about the possibility of a new literary venture – writing novels, and the end of 1813, his publisher Ballantyne's difficulties and the move to Abbotsford provided him with the perfect motivation.

The first *Waverley* chapters (1-8) dealt with political-legal disputes of an English landed family in the early years of the Hanoverians. In Adam Ferguson's language these cover the issues that 'modern' (commercial) society faced with the threats

Chrystal Croftangry notes that his debtor's lodgings were poised between 'the huge city, dark with the smoke of ages and groaning with the sounds of active industry and idle revel, and the lofty and

of 'luxury and corruption', a setting Scott used frequently in his Scottish novels where the progress of civilisation was debated.

The birth and the 'power' of the name *Waverley*: a place, a fictional hero, and the author of *Waverley* himself. We've met Edward, know he's clever, imaginative, rather peculiarly educated. He's plucked out of Surrey and (with no travel description) plonked down in Perthshire:

'He now entered upon a new world, where, for a time, all was beautiful because all was new.'

Start by reading *Waverley's* Chapters VIII-X, and then compare them to the following passage from Scott's'prelude to *The Chronicles of the Canongate* (1827). Chrystal Croftangry, a returned and recovered bankrupt, goes back to his family's old estate in Clydesdale. Concealing his identity, he asks the innkeeper about them and the industrialists who succeeded them and then went bust:

Mair regretted – mair missed? I liked ane of the auld family very weel, but I winna say that for them a'. How should they be mair missed than the Treddleses? The cotton mill was such a thing for the country! The mair bairns

---

craggy hill, silent and solitary as the grave.' They are where the Holyrood Parliament now sits, and resembled the Marshalsea Prison of Charles Dickens' childhood.

---

a cottar body had the better; they would make their awn keep frae the time they were five years auld, and a widow wi three or four bairns was a wealthy woman in the time of the Treddleses.

'But the health of these poor children, my good friend – their education and religious instruction – '

'For health,' said Christie, looking gloomily at me, 'ye maun ken little of the warld, sir, if ye dinna ken that the health of the poor man's body, as well as his youth and his strength, are all at the command of the rich man's purse. There never was a trade so unhealthy yet but men would fight to get wark at it for twa pennies a day aboon the common wage. But the bairns were reasonably weel cared for in the way of air and exercise, and a very responsible youth heard them their Carritch, and gied them lessons in Reediemadeasy. Now, what did they ever get before? Maybe on a winter day they wad be called out to beat the wood for cocks or siclike; and then the starving weans would maybe get a bite of broken bread, and maybe no, just as the butler was in humour —that was a' they got.'

'They were not, then, a very kind family to the

poor, these old possessors?' said I, somewhat bitterly; for I had expected to hear my ancestors' praises recorded, though I certainly'despaired of being regaled with my own.

'They werena ill to them, sir, and that is aye something. They were just decent bien bodies; ony poor creature that had face to beg got an awmous, and welcome – they that were shamefaced gaed by, and twice as welcome. But they keepit an honest walk before God and man, the Croftangrys, and, as I said before, if they did little good, they did as little ill. They lifted their rents, and spent them; called in their kain and ate them; gaed to the kirk of a Sunday; bowed civilly if folk took aff their bannets as they gaed by, and lookit as black as sin at them that keepit them on.'

This comparison makes you sense that Croftangry is a 'modern man' – almost a Victorian social investigator – and what he reports of an 'industrial' society might come out of Carlyle, Dickens or Marx. Edward seems to undergo a quite different experience.

Waverley Chapter VIII is the man talking to you from his own impressions, seeing Tully-Veolan and trying to decode somewhere that appears exotic, like a place from the Italian bit of the Grand Tour, mixed in with Johnson and Boswell's accounts of their 1773 'Highland jaunt'.

At first glance, the place seems chaotic, but very soon Edward senses its real values: vividly different both from Waverley Honour *and* from Croftangry's post-industrial Lanarkshire. Tully-Veolan has its own life and dynamic, where even Daft Davie Gellatley (through his songs and skills as a fisherman) has a place: 'community', if you like, rather than 'organised society'. By Chapter X Edward has 'with much ceremony, and still more real kindness' met his future love Rose, his father-in-law Cosmo Comyn, and Old Scotland, its values, of family, law, learning, good health and love which make the place a sort of Eden.

Contrasting Daft Davie and Cosmo Comyn shows Scott as a professional in what we now call 'oral or folk history', and of law or 'civil history'. He had mastered both disciplines, and as the Irish scholar Owen Dudley Edwards argues in 'Scott as a Contemporary Historian' (*The Long-Forgotten Melody*, 1983) the result justifies the novel as an innovative type of history: getting to the 'marrow' of what people thought about at the time.

PART II
READING AND WRITING
WAVERLEY

'There is no European nation which, within the course of half a century or little more has undergone so complete a change as this kingdom of Scotland . . . but the change, though steadily and rapidly progressive, has nevertheless been gradual; and like those who drift down the stream of a deep and smooth river, we are not aware of the progress we have made until we fix our eye on the point from which we have been drifted.'

Walter Scott, *Waverley*

Courting Rose:
Evan Dhu MacCombich intrigues young Edward
'Ah! If you Saxon Duinhe-wassel saw but the Chief
with his tail on!'

5. The Book of The Year

WHY IN 1814 should the book of the year be *Waverley*, or *'Tis sixty years since*, by an unnamed Scottish author? Why should the adventures of a young Englishman in the last war on British soil, the rising of Prince Charles Edward Stewart in 1745, matter? Causing *Waverley's* fame to rush across the continent, like Harry Potter in our own day, it became recognised as the first 'historical novel' – or at least the first of the type to get to the mainstream.

The author's timing was not calculated, but turned out brilliant. One volume was already complete on 11 April when Napoleon was defeated in Germany and Spain, abdicated and exiled to Elba. The Treaty of Paris officially ended hostilities on 30 May. Scott completed the book in June and *Waverley* went on sale in July. 4,000 copies had been sold by October, when the Congress of Vienna convened. On 26 February 1815 Napoleon escaped from Elba and on 20 March resumed the government of France from Paris, while Scott was being commemorated in

1814-15 were years of unaccustomed travel for Scott. He sailed round Scotland with Robert Stevenson (RLS's grandfather) north to the Shetlands, then via the Hebrides to Portrush in

London by Byron and the Prince Regent. It was as if the events of 1745-6 were replaying on a grand but also personal scale. This ended with the victory of the Allies at Waterloo, near Brussels, on 18 June. Scott was there only five weeks later. He ended the year on 14 December celebrating victory by organising the first, very big, Scottish football match.

Waverley was 'British' as much as Scottish, and diplomatically about unity by agreement rather than conquest. It was considered Shakespearian and in fact closely followed Europe's discovery of Shakespeare, not well known until the German poet Christoph Wieland's first printed translations in the 1750s. Both writers gained great popularity. But what would have happened had Napoleon *won* at Waterloo?

Start out by plunging into the book itself. This isn't always easy. Lots of people get fazed in the very first chapter, by its English setting. (In fact Scott often tends to stuff his first chapters with details about why and how manuscripts turned up in the 'editor's' office, an extended joke better suited to lawyers and historians). The advice: skip to the point where the hero gets on his horse; though later on you can find yourself coming back to 'our editor' to check up.

Ulster. During this trip he took notes to supply
William Daniell with information for his famous
series of acquatints. In late summer he visited
Brussels and Paris.

At this stage you might find it useful to divide the
novel into sections – and five or six of these 'blocks'
suggest themselves. Work out how long they take in
chronological terms (relating this to the development
of 'the crisis') and how they progress the action.

The novel's narrative is in fact presented like the
Cantos of Scott's narrative poems, with roughly
similarly-sized sections, from the English manor-
house up to the politicking at the Jacobite court in
Edinburgh. The Cantos were usually based on 'scene-
setting' as in Shakespeare's plays, and this fairly
static form governs the first two-thirds of the book.
Thereafter the action is in shorter bursts of activity:

I-VI
– at Waverley Honour, 43 pages

VII-XV
– at Bradwardine's Tully-Veolan, 51 pages

XVI-XXVIII
– at Fergus MacIvor's Glennaquoich, 58 pages

XXIX; Vol II, I-X
– Waverley captive, central Scotland, 61 pages

XI-XXVII
– Court at Holyrood, battle of Prestonpans, 80 pages

An element of enjoying the story lies in sharing Edward Waverley's doubts, quandaries and bafflement, though if the puzzlement gets too much for you, fast-forward to the section where Rose Bradwardine settles the facts that have determined his wanderings.

The young Englishman is faced with a doubtful inheritance, a divided and unfriendly family, and opponents to his own cause. We start off from 'modern times' when the 'big' people are more interested in money and London politics, to travel with our hero back in time to older and more contested regions.

Is Edward Waverley like the guy in the Western movie getting off the stagecoach at the frontier town and running into customs and relationships that are surprising and dangerous? Yes, and for Edward, these get more perilous when he moves northwards from Tully-Veolan to Glennaquoich and the altogether more emotional appeal of the Highland chief Fergus MacIvor and his sister Flora.

But what sort of novel is *Waverley*? Leave these questions open as Edward leaves for the Highlands. Remember that Scott said he used his plots 'simply to bring good things on'. Remember his Edinburgh friends seeing him in his Castle Street window, writing *Waverley*, working ceaselessly and apparently automatically on his four hundred pages:

A romantic melodrama? The Highlands appear at their scenic best, and on cue the Highlanders hunt and rally and intrigue and fight.

A comedy? The greatest danger Edward runs at Tully-Veolan is wrecking his liver!

A political intrigue? Fergus is traditional chief at Glennaquoich, a schemer in Holyrood.

A farce? Edward's loyalty is put under suspicion because the Army takes his tutor's Jacobite tosh seriously.

A tragedy? Romantic Fergus will die William Wallace's horrible death at Carlisle, along with Evan Maccombich, his loyal kinsman.

A romance? Rose Bradwardine, smitten (a bit, anyway) by Edward, gets him out of trouble, and they live happily ever after.

Do all these elements somehow cohere, because of Scott's wealth of plot and descriptive skill? Inventive comedy is balanced with a careful appeal to the feelings, rather like the way he handles adventure, romance and sex in *Young Lochinvar*.

Is Fergus's death a tragedy? He's captured in a minor skirmish at Clifton, not slain at Culloden. There's no spectacular set-piece. Defiance is left to Evan. John Buchan thought this a 'subtler and more beautiful rhythm' quite new among poor men. Offered mercy if he rejects his chief, Evan answers:

> 'If the Saxon gentlemen are laughing because a poor man, such as me, thinks my life, or the life of six of my degree, is worth that of Vich Ian Vohr, it's like enough they may be very right; but if they laugh because they think I would not keep my word, and come back to redeem him, I can tell them they ken

neither the heart of a Hielander, nor the
honour of a gentleman.
'Grace me no grace. Since you are to shed
Vich Ian Vohr's blood, the only favour I would
accept from you is to bid them loose my
hands and gie me my claymore, and bide you
just a minute sitting where ye are!'

The action of *Waverley* isn't fanciful but likely to
occur in a large-scale war, like that of 1793-1814.
Many Britons saw action, and found themselves
fighting their own kin, as in America (1776-83) and
in 1812. People 'out there' were similarly placed to
Scott and his readers: on a Border, meeting 'the
exotic' and having to come to terms with it.

Reading *Waverley*, Scott's early style can be
ponderous and affect the speech of his characters.
But compared with other writers, his *clichés* are few;
you read faster than you think; and you look in detail
at the scenes presented.

6. Waverley's Life and Times

IN 1814, *Waverley's* themes were vitalised by the coincidence of 'Scott-land' with political and technical upheaval. The French Wars didn't just end spectacularly in East Europe and the Peninsula, in Napoleon they left a heroic figure who altered Europe in immense ways, from language and measurement, to politics, nationalism and tourism.

Consider the impact of the age on Scotland. The country's popularity was partly down to aristocrats not being able to take their traditional 'Grand Tour' of the Continent. Getting north was helped by technical innovations: bringing Scotland within two days of London. In 1745 it had been a fortnight.

Edward Waverley's 'schools' are the 'residences' of Waverley Honour, Tully-Veolan, Glennaquoich, and Holyrood which together make up about the first half of the book. They are described in great detail and we may find this a bit much – photography came in only a decade after Scott's death but took time to evict the descriptive purple prose.

Scott combined and conveyed three things: his ability to present a well-chosen landscape, his skill as a lyricist, and his ability to cleverly compress large sections of text. The first came from growing up with the disciplines of geology and physical geography. The second reads lessons from landscape: the image of water, or of Highland freedom. The third brings economy: as in the *Coronach* (dirge) for a clansman killed in his long poem *The Lady of the Lake* (1811):

> He is gone on the mountain.
> He is lost to the forest
> Like a summer-dried fountain,
> When our need was the sorest.
> The font, reappearing,
> From the rain-drops shall borrow,
> But to us comes no cheering,
> To Duncan no morrow.

In fact, a good way of approaching *Waverley* is to read *The Lady of the Lake*. It's set in the mid-16th century in the 'miniature Highlands' of the Trossachs 30km to the west of Stirling and shares much of *Waverley*'s scenery. Tully-Veolan and Glennaquoich are supposed to be in Perthshire, but the country of

Scott's scenery was painted by the greatest of the day, JMW Turner, and this greatly influenced the art critic, John Ruskin, master of the 'purple passage'

Fergus MacIvor is what Scott was familiar with, around Aberfoyle.

Scenery is important because the South Highlands 'read' both at a distance and close up. At the time of *Waverley's* publication, they were easier to get to than the Borders, and are marked by three great mountains – Ben Lomond, Ben Ledi and Ben Venue – visible from much of central Scotland, but set back from the south by a tract of flat marshy land.

The pathos of *Coronach* contrasts with the often brutal conduct of monarchs and clan chiefs in the last years of Catholic Scotland, 1541-60 – the dying phase of the Auld Alliance with France. In fact *The Lady* and *Waverley* bracket the Anglo-Scottish drama which 'contained' the House of Stewart.

You can 'frame' the writing of *Waverley* between two dates. In 1799, Cardinal Henry Stewart, the last Pretender, was pensioned by George III. In 1822, Scott organised 'the Royal jaunt' for George IV, who was unpopular in London. He dug out the Scots Crown Jewels from a cellar in Edinburgh Castle and presided over 'a gathering of the Gael' giving the royal family their taste for Highland exoticism.

of descriptive prose. When photography started in
the early 1840s, early photogrpahers imitated
Turner's scenes when recording 'Scott's Scotland'.

In 1827-8 he wrote the history of Scotland as *Tales of a Grandfather* to entertain his grandson Johnie Lockhart, who was often ill. Chapters 75-87, nearly 100 close-type pages, cover the Rebellion of 1745-6. Two short stories of this time, 'The Highland Widow' and 'The Two Drovers' are dark, powerful studies of Highlanders trapped in the new order and destroyed by it.

PART III
IN-LAWS AND OUTLAWS,
OR FAMILIES,
CLANS AND CRIME

'Like the Homeric Greeks they were cruel, coarse savages, slaying each other as beasts of the forest, and yet they were also poets who could express in the grand style the inexorable fate of the individual man and woman, the infinite pity for all the cruel things which they none the less perpetually inflicted on one another. . . If the people had not loved the songs, many of the best would have perished. The Border Ballads, for good and for evil, express this society and its quality of mind.'

G.M. Trevelyan,
The Middle Marches (1914)

Carlisle: Fergus's farewell
'This same law of high treason, Edward, is one of the
blessings of your free country. . .
But what a dying man can suffer firmly, may kill a living
friend to look upon.'

7. 'Thae were gude days on the Border. . .'

IN A 'PEEL TOWER' on the eve of Union in 1707, Jacobite and auld reiver malcontents assemble.

'Our commerce is destroyed,' hollowed old John Rewcastle, a Jedburgh smuggler, from the lower end of the table.

'Our agriculture is ruined,' said the Laird of Broken-girth-flow, a territory which, since the days of Adam, had borne nothing but ling and whortle-berries.

'Our religion is cut up, root and branch,' said the pimple-nosed pastor of the Episcopal meeting-house at Kirkwhistle.

'We shall shortly neither dare shoot a deer nor kiss a wench, without a certificate from the presbytery and kirk-treasurer,' said Mareschal-Wells.

'Or make a brandy jeroboam in a frosty

morning, without licence from a commissioner of excise,' said the smuggler.

'Or ride over the fell in a moonless night,' said Westburnflat, 'without asking leave of young Earnscliff; or some Englified justice of the peace: thae were gude days on the Border when there was neither peace nor justice heard of.'

Marechal Wells (a sort of crooked sheriff) in Scott's novella *The Black Dwarf* (1816) reminds us how new statute law was on his native heath. What he satirises is the customary law of the Border families or 'graynes' and the Scots nobles' 'heritable jurisdictions' which ended after the 1745 rising.

This is broad comedy. *Waverley* ends in understated, offstage horror. Fergus and Evan Maccombich will be slowly torn to pieces on the gallows of Carlisle: everyone knew what 'hanging, drawing and quartering' meant.

On 22 September 1814, the first of many statues to Scottish patriot William Wallace was unveiled, commissioned by the Earl of Buchan overlooking the beautiful ruin of Dryburgh where Scott would be buried. 'Great Patriot Hero: Ill-Requited Chief!': the fact that its inscription came from an earlier Border poet, James Thomson of Ednam, who also wrote 'Rule Britannia!' should make us wary of notions that the Union was, even at its zenith, totally inclusive.

What happened to the 'reivers' of the debateable land? They were the people whose folktales Scott had collected as a young man in Liddesdale, a remote pastoral region two days ride from Edinburgh.

After the 1770s the Borderers rapidly changed, becoming 'scientific' in farming and manufacturing, with an important woollen industry: though transport remained difficult even in Scott's heyday. Hence his interest in railways, schemes to connect the region to Glasgow and Berwick in 1811-14, to Edinburgh and the Lothian coalfield in 1821.

'Reivers' who didn't fit in migrated to the Highlands and Ulster, to East Europe, and via such routes to the New World and the Orient, carrying various sorts of 'bare-knuckle' enterprise with them. They were frontiersmen, and they tended to define themselves 'by the other'.

Baron Bradwardine, says Scott, 'might remind a modern of the days of zealous volunteer service, when the bar-gown of our pleaders was often flung over a blazing uniform.'

In the 1960s, Professor Nicholas Phillipson used punchcard computing to analyse the eighteenth-century Faculty of Advocates. These Edinburgh lawyers were mainly from landed society, perhaps regarding legal processes as 'a continuation of clan warfare by other means'. Feudal law really mattered in Scotland, its teacher being Scott's friend Baron David Hume of Godscroft, nephew of his philosopher namesake, 'Godless Davie'. His lectures were the basis of Scots feudal law into our own day.

Law transformed society from being linked by habit and '*kind*liness'. In Scotland this meant being regulated by an elaborate legal framework. The Kirk busied itself with education, poverty and social discipline, Parliament House (the law) with inherit-ance, patronage, infrastructure, even economic policy.

8. Chiefs, Families and Houses

SCOTT DESCRIBED the property of a laird as 'a tower-hoose, a midden, an' a guid-gangin' plea.' The first was a place of safety against casual violence and robbery, sheltering wife and kin, while her man roamed Europe behind a foreign drum. The second showed he had cattle, horses and livestock. The third provided the excuse for travelling to Edinburgh for law, politics, sex and above all drink.

Ceremonial lawsuits bound the 'estaites of the nation' – local government, kirk, universities, and private morality – by and to the law. Covenants reinforced Scottish identity where religion might divide it.

Scott's life was divided between the City of Edinburgh – representing perhaps Europe's fastest urbanisation – and the Border countryside: two contrasting areas of activity. Here landlords were at work, enclosing common land, improving crop-yield

'Abbotsford . . . my Conundrum Castle'
'He was living in his ancestral countryside like a little king
. . . if the dream was baseless,
it was assuredly not ignoble.' *John Buchan*

and livestock, from grand houses like the Duke of Buccleuch's Bowhill or the Duke of Roxburghe's Floors. This was a combination of feudal power, capital and science, and foreign involvement. It seems also to have drawn on the capacity of extended families to protect and nurture the 'lad o' pairts', as the Franco-Scots scholar Emanuel Todd has argued in *The Causes of Progress* (1989).

Scott was one of several remarkable figures of this type, and knew it. In *Guy Mannering* (1815) he sketches the Edinburgh in which as an English visitor wrote, 'I can, in a few minutes, take fifty men of genius and learning by the hand'. But he also stressed the balance with the land.

Compare Scott's career with that of the achieve-ment of his associates James Hogg and John Leyden, both sons of Border shepherds. Combining a grasp of science with imagination, Hogg mastered the clinical psychology of the time, while Leyden pushed to the limit the definitions of clergyman, judge, academic, administrator, orientalist in an adult life of scarcely twenty years. Scot mourned him in *The Lord of the Isles*:

> Scenes sung by him who sings no more:
> His bright and brief career is o'er,

Melrose didn't follow Scotland's move to
manufacturing. Linen and cotton-weaving closed
down after 1815, but it became a home for well-to-
do professionals and the retired. Building at the yard

And mute his tuneful strains;
Quenched is his lamp of varied lore,
That loved the light of song to pour,
A distant and a deadly shore
Has Leyden's cold remains.

What effect, overall, did improvement and
patronage have? Unquestionably it increased the
law's prestige, made it more business-like. See the
grand legal portraits of Sir Henry Raeburn and
contrast them with the Whig advocate Henry
Cockburn's acid sketches, in *Memorials of his Time*
(1856).

Scott's own 'utopia' Abbotsford seems to fit in here,
reminding us that Robert Owen's New Lanark (which
Scott rather approved of) was only fifty miles away.
The house was to have been a classical cottage, then
Scott Gothicised it, elaborating a design by William
Atkinson, a rather odd combination of Tudor
mansion and Scottish hall, designed around his
collection of relics and ideas.

Abbotsford had the spirit of Tully-Veolan, but was
gaslit, large-windowed, integrated with its gardens –
and quite undefendable. Scott prided himself that
the Border folk could wander round 'the policies'.

of the Smith brothers in Darnick became the biggest industry with 80 workers. The Smiths built much of Abbotsford, villas in Melrose and Gattonside, and in 1814 the Wallace Statue above Dryburgh.

Waverley opened out Scotland as somewhere to be seen and Abbotsford – originally a rather bleak and exposed farm amid treeless hills and next to a difficult ford across the Tweed – blossomed. First as a Gothic 'armoury' wing to the old farmhouse (1814-17), then after the success of *Ivanhoe* in 1820 as a grand design combining library, study, Chinese drawing room and dining room, set in formal gardens and surrounded by trees planted to resemble Wellington's battle array at Waterloo.

Scott couldn't have predicted that his financial fall in January 1826 would make Abbotsford his only residence. He determined to pay off his debts, which seemed unrealistic. Many of his friends would have forgiven a bankruptcy. But he crossed his own party by a 'flyting'. *The Letters of Malachi Malagrowther* defended the Scots right to issue their own banknotes. It wasn't a conceit: Scott had an almost pre-Keynesian view about growth depending on the money supply – and found himself cast off by his political patrons.

He left Castle Street, Edinburgh on 15 March, and two months later his wife Charlotte died of cancer:

'Cerements of lead and of wood already hold her; cold earth must have her soon. . . they

are arranging the chamber of death; that
which was long the apartment of connubial
happiness. They are treading fast and thick.
For weeks you could have heard a foot-fall.
Oh my God!'

The *Journal* turned out almost the best of late
Scott. But the two bleak stories that Croftangry
introduces: 'The Highland Widow' and 'The Two
Drovers' and his 'Introduction', are rightly comm-
ended by John Buchan:

'He paints in finer strokes and in quieter
tints, but with an economy and certainty
which recall some of the best work of
Turgenev. The ebbing of the current of life
seems to have left him with clearer eyes.'

Finer strokes in quieter tints had grown as part of
Scott's own character long before, as in one of the
first poems he collected, 'The Border Widow's
lament':

My love he built me a bonnie bow'r,
And clad it all with lilie flow'r;
A brawer bow'r ye ne'er did see,
Than my true love he built for me.

There came a man, by middle day,
He spied his sport and went away;
And brought the king that very night,
Who brake my bow'r and slew my knight.

He slew my knight, to me sae dear;
He slew my knight, and poined his gear;
My servants all for life did flee,
And left me in extremitie.

Nae living man I'll love again,
Since that my lovely knight is slain;
With ae lock of his yellow hair
I'll chain my heart for ever mair.

Scott did not go quietly. He remained a Tory
partisan and the progress of Whig reform appalled
him. Yet these last stories and the 'meanings' built
into Abbotsford by Croftangry (*croft-an-ri*, or 'king's
field' in Gaelic) and the *Journal* seem to show the
answer to the question posed by the great German
novelist Theodor Fontane, 'What would we know of
Scotland without Scott?' Which he answered with:
'The spontaneous poetry of a people mirrors its entire
culture.'

9. Law and Money

ABBOTSFORD wasn't a retreat. Scott had maybe sympathised with the French revolution for a matter of weeks in 1789, but was always a strong political conservative. Yet he regarded himself as a Scottish patriot – 'You will destroy and undermine until nothing of what makes Scotland Scotland will remain'. He was otherwise an innovator. He directed the Edinburgh Oil-Gas Company; Abbotsford was gas-lit. He opposed slavery, backed Catholic rights, steamboats and iron bridges. Between 1811-1821 he unsuccessfully projected railways to Glasgow, Edinburgh and Berwick.

His Glasgow merchant Nicol Jarvie in *Rob Roy* lauded the Union for gaining him a Jamaican plantation by 1715. There were eleven Waverlys (sic) and five Melroses in the USA by the 1870s , and much Scottish cash was being invested there. In 1848 James Hope Scott, who had married Sir Walter's grand-daughter, inherited Abbotsford. He made his fortune by being Britain's most expert railway lawyer.

A year later the line reached Melrose. Railway law was a way through which Scots businessmen found themselves opening up the American west, as Robert Louis Stevenson would record when he crossed the USA in the 1880s.

Yet the reivers (Border and American) had a 'mobility' that didn't quite fit 'civil society'. William Faulkner was another regional conservative but in his last novel *The Reivers* (1962) the car takes over – just when the cowboy rode into Hollywood. Compare cars in later American and Scots crime stories and movies: four legs good, four wheels better.

Scotland had earlier played an important role in America's Episcopal Church. It was in communion with Canterbury, like the Scottish 'piskies' to whom Scott unenthusiastically belonged. Self-governing, with a Jacobite past, it ordained 'rebel' clergy. An outlaw act? Possibly, but it surely fitted 'the law of nature and of nations'.

The 'reivers' (robbers) – the word is common to Scotland and the US - were still not integrated into civil society. Scott accepted that authors would always be robbed 'over there' by US publishers, even if, as Selkirk sheriff, he was like an American lawman.

In 1794-96 the Borderer Gilbert Elliot, Lord Minto, ran Corsica, Viceroy of Britain's least-known Union. Before 14th July 1789, Bonaparte had wanted to join Minto's partner, Pasquale Paoli. One of history's great 'What ifs'?

If his predecessors failed to ensure that law was enforced they were quite remote from aid at barracks in Edinburgh Castle or Berwick. There wasn't a network of military roads as in the Highlands. Scott's fears at the end of his life at being 'burked' (lynched) by radicals weren't completely neurotic. His final voyage, paid for by his opponents, the Whigs, might have been a decent gesture and a clever precaution.

'The Sons of the Father', from Balzac to Turgenev
'They were right to erect that monument to Scott.' George
Simenon said, 'He invented us all. Without him none of us
could have written as we do.'
Allan Massie

PART IV
SCOTT AND EUROPE

'Why should I not do for Swabian history,
for the rivers and valleys of the Alb, what
Walter Scott has done for the Borders and
the Tweed?'

Wilhelm Hauff prefaces
Lichtenstein, 1825

10. Nation Building

EVEN IN THE MIDDLE AGES, disease (such as the Black Death) or new aristocratic fads reached Scotland as fast as a horse or sailing ship could carry them. Understand this when looking at *Waverley's* remarkable success.

The years 1803-14 had seen the whole of Europe in turmoil, the Holy Roman Empire broken up in 1806, and Russia invaded in 1812 when Napoleon's power stretched from Moscow to Gibraltar. If a book was going to take a continent – and other places – by storm, 1814 was the right year to do it.

Britain was now top nation, not having been invaded or broken up, and expanded by forcing Union on Ireland in 1801. The Brtish were also due to mend fences with the USA after the 1812 war, symbolised by the 'Columbia Press' of 1814: a high-speed cast-iron hand-press crowned by an American eagle – in fact a very efficient counterweight. On the

Columbia Press, many sheets of Scott's works would be turned out, as well as the growing numbers of literary or political reviews and local newspapers, usually weekly or twice-weekly. *The London Times*, a daily since 1785, was now printed by steam power.

Ironically, Scott's books would circulate because the Irish-Americans had become efficient literary pirates, producing cheap editions on which they paid no royalties. He acted the role-model for American writers like Washington Irving and Fenimore Cooper.

Post-Napoleonic war, a huge market opened up, and innovations ranged from cheap paper to afford-able spectacles and gaslight in place of tallow candles. The patriotism of ordinary people had been a weapon in the fight against the French. It was payback time.

Scott was a literary capitalist, but he had yet to break into this world. He did so in 1819, after a severe illness changed his writing style, temporarily, to dictation. The result was his most successful novel *Ivanhoe*. It was often abridged, 'chapbooked', and filmed, and was the second of the famous *Classics Illustrated* comics. It ran by 1914 into over seventy editions compared with *Waverley's* twenty three. It also paid.

> Does there seem to be a link between success in
> war and intellectual reputation? Do Congresses
> like Vienna and emergencies like Napoleon's

John Buchan regarded Scott's medievalism as 'an inferior lode', but it still carried from the Scottish novels an interest in the clash of societies and the power of minorities: the Jews in this case, later in *The Talisman*, the Moslems.

Yet capitalism helped. In France, Honore de Balzac, a bohemian monarchist of enormous literary and sexual energy, gripped by Scott's narrative poems and *Ivanhoe*, took on the medieval romance as an enterprise, closely followed by Victor Hugo, whose *Notre Dame de Paris* (1831) virtually replicated Scott's plot. Alexandre Dumas' romances fitted in here. Stendhal, Napoleonist and liberal, viewed Scott sceptically – too laborious in his prose, stiflingly proper and chaste – but accepted the scale of his achievement.

In Europe, the problem was that as 'the author of *Waverley*' was still uncredited, impostures were possible. *Walladmor* and *Schloss Avalon* were passed off as German translations in 1825, by a young writer 'Willibald Alexis' (G.W. Haering), a perceptive Scott critic.

Scott aided, but would be eclipsed by, the career of the Grimm brothers, who published their first 'Tales' in 1812 and Wilhelm Hauff (1802-27) who wrote countless tales as remarkable as the Grimms

'Hundred Days' (20 March – 8 July 1815) draw
people together?

---

and in 1826 a long novel about the reformation in
Swabia called *Lichtenstein* (consciously modelled on
Old Mortality). Hauff persuaded the King to rebuild
Schloss Lichtenstein as what it *ought* to have looked
like: Abbotsford perched on the edge of a 600 foot
drop.

Goethe placed *Waverley* 'alongside the best things
that had ever been written', but warmed more to
Ivanhoe (he had problems with Scots dialect). The
German poet, novelist, and travel writer Theodor
Fontane (1819-98) and Karl Marx (1819-82) were
both devotees. Karl Marx's wife Jenny was part
Campbell, while Georg Lukacs (1885-1971), the
Hungarian Marxist theoretician/politician wrote *The
Historical Novel* (1938) which revived interest in
Scott.

Italy, united under the Bonapartes, was divided
after 1815. Its leading poet, Alessandro Manzoni,
inspired by *Ivanhoe*, set a novel of love and tyranny
The Betrothed (1825) in the Spanish tyranny of 1628
in Lombardy. It didn't just attack invaders and
landlords and show the courage of its young,
commoner, hero and heroine; the purity of its Tuscan
made it the preferred Italian literary language. It was
still compulsory in Italian schools in the 1990s.

In Russia, Scott's *Life of Napoleon* gave him official contacts, despite a failure to get through to the rather dim Tsar Alexander I in Paris. He influenced Russian writers, notably Alexander Pushkin in his novel *The Captain's Daughter* (1836).

Later on would come the formidable achievements of Scandinavian and Russian drama, from Ibsen to Turgenev and Chekhov: one foot in an 'epical past' the other in current, often revolutionary, politics.

These built on other influences – the habit of Scots serving abroad, notably in Russia and East Europe, and in the places frequented by Grand Tourists: the Mediterranean or Spanish cities, the German spas, and the great bohemian capital of Paris.

The small palace of Laxenburg, about 10 km east of Vienna was built up by the Habsburgs as a gothic theme park: the influence of *Ivanhoe* to be seen in jousting lists, a moated castle. Scott mania boomed before the revolutions of 1848 when conservatives like Frederick William IV of Prussia tried prog- rammes of conservative reform and religious revival. After the 1848 revolution these were repeated, but Scott's influence went left, with Marx seeing him as the prophet of the harsh economic polarisation of the capitalist age. This was the age of 'realism' in which novelists used apparently 'rounded' characters to demonstrate moral conflicts and largely argue for reform. By the 1860s, particularly in France, 'naturalism' had taken over, with 'free will' and individuality diminished in the novels of Flaubert and Zola.

PART V
SCOTT ON THE STAGE

'I went to see that amusement in its birthplace, which is now so widely received over Europe. The Opera House is superb, but can seldom be quite full. On this night, however, it was; the guards, citizens, and all persons dependent on the Court are expected to take places liberally, and applaud with spirit.'

Walter Scott, Teatro San Carlo,
Naples, 1831

Scottswomen from the stalls
Ellen in Rossini's *La Donna del Lago;*
Edith/Elvira in Bellini's *I Puritani;*
Lucia, very mad, in Donizetti's *Lucia di Lammermoor;*
Catarina in Bizet's *La Jolie Fille de Perth*

11. 'What's Opera, Scott?'

THIS HEADING was cheekily borrowed from the famous Looney Tunes cartoon of 1937 'What's Opera, Doc?', a six-minute version of Wagner's Ring cycle (16 hours!) starring Bugs Bunny. It makes the point: parody is educational as well as fun, and confirms the line of T.S. Eliot: 'Bad poets borrow. Great poets steal.'

Scott started in drama: radicalism of a sort in Scotland, as plays had been frowned on since the Reformation. His adaptation of Goethe's *Goetz von Berlichingen: 'Ironhand'* brings on the 'man in the middle' dilemma of *Waverley*, though the stage proved too limited.

Rob Roy was dramatised immediately as it had scenery (roughly the same as *Waverley*'s), a melodramatic plot, a finger-lickin'-nasty villain in Rashleigh Osbaldistone, Die Vernon as witty heroine and Bailie Nicol Jarvie as comic lead. It was still playing in 1917. This demonstrates how Scott's

---

Think of the novels you're currently reading. How would you adapt them for the stage? Which parts would you keep, and which would you remove?

---

works could be drastically adapted but still enhance the original.

In 1819, Scott hit the opera stage when Gioachino Rossini, Director of Naples' San Carlo from 1815, launched his *Lady of the Lake*. It was a success both in Naples and the USA, where one song 'Hail to the Chief!' (though with different music) became the Presidential Anthem. Scored by Franz Schubert, its 'Ave Maria' is still a soprano showpiece. Other Scott operas would follow.

Scott's own view of the Naples Opera wasn't over-whelming:

> 'The Opera bustled off without any
> remarkable music, and, so far as I
> understand the language, no poetry; and
> except the 'coup d'œil', which was
> magnificent, it was poor work. . . I came
> home at half-past nine, without waiting the
> ballet, but I was dog-sick of the whole of it.'

Naples in 1800 was the third-largest city in Europe with a population of 426,000 (London one million, Paris 600,000). It had the world's oldest Opera House, opened in 1737, when music culture spread from the courts to the cities. La Scala, Milan followed

'What's Opera, Scott?'

> What are the differences between a successful story
> on the stage, and on the page or on film?

in 1776, La Fenice, Venice, in 1792, Theatre Royal,
Covent Garden in 1808. The vast buildings of Vienna
in 1869 and Paris in 1875, were steam-age, rivalled
by the Teatro Massimo, built at Palermo in 1897 for
the new rich of industrial Europe who flocked to Italy
by means ranging from steam yacht to the famous
excursions organised by Thomas Cook. Opera
became as much part of cultural capitalism based
on the novel as the station bookstall or public library.

The old European monarchies had to steer a
course between three forces: economic change, revolutionary patriotism and the great powers represented
by Metternich and his Congresses.

Scott had shown, by stage-managing George IV's
visit to Edinburgh in 1822, how spectacle could
present the old order in a good light. Opera houses
were central to an urban middle-class culture which
lacked representative government, resented
repression yet feared the disruption of industry and
city growth.

Scott's Naples debut turned out to be the first of
twenty-five Italian operas based on his works. Jerome
Mitchell's *The Walter Scott Operas* (1975) details
upwards of fifty in Europe. Such entertainments

bought off radicalism. But they kept a bohemian, artistic community going which could turn volatile.

12. Song, Sex and Violence

S AN CARLO is still going strong, looking much as it did in the early 1800s. Even Scott's critic, Stendhal approved *La Donna* at its 1819 premiere. Rossini's hummable music made him a huge success in Naples and his mistress, Isabella Colbran sang the part of Ellen. Another important vocalist was Maria Malibran, 'the Diva of the Romantic Age', who excelled in the near-obligatory 'mad scene', the finest of which was in *Lucia di Lammermoor*.

Gaetano Donizetti of Bergamo took his version of Scott's *The Bride of Lammermoor* to Naples in 1835, the year Vincenzo Bellini of Catania died, just as his *I Puritani* conquered Paris and London. Bellini adapted a French play *Roundheads and Cavaliers*, which transferred *Old Mortality*'s action from the Clyde Valley in the late 1670s to the siege of Plymouth in the English Civil War in 1649. It was a favourite of Queen Victoria, a fan of the *Waverley Novels*, and of her Albert.

Bellini was a dashing, radical dandy, praised by

Scott's English or medieval novels have always
been more popular as films than his Scottish
stories, although most people regard the latter as

'Harry' Heine, German-Jewish, pro-British as a
Hanoverian subject, and radical friend of Karl Marx.
He grew up in a Sicily ruled 'constitutionally' by the
English Whig Lord William Bentinck, an early
enthusiast for Italian unity. *I Puritani* focussed on
the 'Scott hero' torn between the two sides, ultimately
abandoning the Royalists for safety and love. As
staged, it enabled the unlikely Puritans to embody
musically the notion of national freedom.

Opera was dangerous stuff. George Meredith's
novel *Vittoria* (1867) had a soprano lead revolution
in 1848. See Luchino Visconti's grand historical film
Senso of 1954, which starts with a demonstration at
a performance of Verdi's Scott-influenced *Trovatore*
(1853) in Venice on the eve of the Austro-Italian war
of 1866.

The French were also enthused. Berlioz composed
his overtures 'Les Franc-Juges' (vaguely related to
Scott's version of Goethe's *Goetz von Berlichingen*
followed by *Waverley* and *Rob Roy*.

'The French Mozart' Francois-Adrien Boieldieu's
La Dame Blanche of 1825 pasted together bits from
The Abbot, *The Monastery* and *Guy Mannering* and
used real Scots folk-songs. A great success in Paris,
La Dame influenced Bellini and Donizetti, and

better. *Bonnie Prince Charlie* (1948) with David
Niven, was a turkey. Peter Walkins' *Culloden* is
reckoned rightly, brilliant but harrowing.

Georges Bizet's *The Fair Maid of Perth* in 1861.

Felix Mendelssohn came to Scotland in 1829, failed
to see Scott, but his Hebrides Overture (1830) and
later Scottish Symphony were then composed.

Even Richard Wagner had the *Waverley Novels*
on his bookshelf at his very bourgeois Villa Wahnfried
(the name means 'quiet after madness'!) at Bayreuth.

In Britain the novels generated many ballad-
operas, mainly by Sir Henry Bishop. Few have
survived, even Sir Arthur Sullivan's name couldn't
keep his *Ivanhoe* (1891) on stage. The Scot Hamish
MacCunn tried *The Lay of the Last Minstrel* and
Jeannie Deans with little better luck. Why the
failure?

The British equivalent already existed in the combination of the theatrical pantomime and the political
novel, both of which take off from Scott, Galt and
Disraeli. The pantomime has melodrama – 'Look
who's behind you!' – incredible plots, glamorous
hero/heroines (both played by girls) and the novel
equals the grand opera chorus and ensemble in its
election scenes.

PART VI
SCOTT, SCOTLAND AND THE USA

'Sir Walter made every gentleman in the South a Major or a Colonel, or a General or a Judge, before the war. . . he created rank and caste down there, and also reverence for rank and caste, and pride and pleasure in them. Sir Walter had so large a hand in making Southern character, as it existed before the war, that he is in great measure responsible for the war. . .'

Mark Twain,
Life on the Mississippi (1883)

13. The Flyting With Twain

THE CENTENARY of Mark Twain's death and the 240th anniversary of Scott's birth were marked in 2011. This coincided with the effects of Hurricane Katrina laying-up the Glasgow-built *Delta Queen*, the last of the river paddle-steamers that had been Twain's 'schoolrooms'. In *Life on the Mississippi* (1883). Twain, born Sam Clemens in 1835, let fly at Scott:

> 'He did measureless harm; more real and lasting harm, perhaps, than any other individual that ever wrote. Most of the world has now outlived good part of these harms. . . but in our South they flourish pretty forcefully still. There, the genuine and wholesome civilisation of the nineteenth century is curiously confused and commingled with the Walter Scott Middle-Age sham civilisation; and so you have practical, common-sense, progressive ideas, and progressive works; mixed up with the duel, the inflated speech, and the *jejeune*

romanticism of an absurd past that is dead.
But for the Sir Walter disease, the character
of the Southerner – or Southron, according to
Sir Walter's starchier way of phrasing it –
would be wholly modern. . .'

Though, as Hollywood rather fancied 'tushery', this probably did Scott's reputation no harm. Remember Roger Moore swashing his buckle in the small-screen *Further Adventures of Ivanhoe*? – 'Ivanhoe! Ivanhoe! He's bold, he's brave, he's gay!'

Twain's assault is what Scots call 'flyting': a tradition going back to the first 'Makars'. Like military dancing, flyting is aggressive: verbal displays and vicious insults being inflicted, often in desperate days. Flyting is linked to Scots skill in journalism and cartooning: Byron's satire 'English Bards and Scotch Reviewers' of the 1800s was matched by the acid-dipped pens of Scots caricaturists such as John Kay, George Cruikshank and James Gillray.

Twain seems to blame Scott for superficialities. A historian might see the slave economy and its expansion, the divergence of economic systems: protectionist, industrial North versus cotton-exporting South, or the potency of 'States Rights'

The American South was not economically backward.
The steam-powered South Carolina Railroad at
Charleston opened only 3 months after the Liverpool
and Manchester in 1830. By then there were also 1200
steamers mainly on the Mississippi River system after

against federal unity. These brought on perhaps the
most destructive conflict of the nineteenth century,
which had its own effect on southern consciousness.

Does Twain deploy what Alfred Hitchcock called a
'McGuffin' here? A plot-device intended to mislead?
He had his own defending to do, being as wayward a
literary earner as Scott (and in rather the same writer/
innovator/entrepreneur group). Besides his own
money problems, and dodgy speculations, was he
trying to save the reputation of one Civil War hero,
Ulysses S. Grant? Twain published Grant's *Memoirs*
and saved the latter's fortune and reputation in 1885-
6, even though Grant as an ineffective President
(1868-77), had allowed much of the 'Gilded Age' of
Washington corruption to happen, about which Twain
loudly complained.

In 1877, Confederate ex-President Jefferson Davis,
at liberty since 1867, visited the United Kingdom and
took the train to Abbotsford. Twain got a great chance
to let rip at Scott, though he could have learned from
and empathised with someone rather similar.

Both Scott and Twain had a strong, ironic sense
of humour; both lived with a striking landscape

their introduction by the Scots-American Robert Fulton in 1811, a year before Henry Bell in Scotland. The problem was that economic growth depended on black slaves, 40% of the Southern population; in South Carolina 67%. Walter Scott was a consistent opponent of slavery.

(much more dangerous for the river pilot Twain). Both loved new technology (*Life on the Mississippi* was the first typewritten manuscript) and both were hit by financial failure.

In fact, it might be more accurate to see Scott, and *Waverley* in particular, as influential in the expansion of the United States. The brief but fierce Anglo-American war came to an end in December 1814, and there was no further military conflict. The exploitation of the 'new golden land' of the Mississippi, the Prairies and the Rockies for cotton, meat, leather, gold was to a great extent up to the 1860s propelled by British demand, investment and settlers.

For a new generation of American writers, such as Longfellow and Emerson, Scott's handling of social variety and change in his poems and novels – conveyed by such friends as Washington Irving – passed into American tradition, both directly and through important studies like the Scott fan Alexis de Tocqueville in his book *Democracy in America* (1837).

14. Chivalry:
Its Cause and Cure

MARK TWAIN attacked the courtly, chivalrous element in 'Southron' upper-class style. But by this word, Scott meant 'English,' not the USA's South. This was also Scott's own interpretation in *Ivanhoe* and *The Talisman* (both critical of the aristocracy and revolted by the Crusaders).

Scott recognised how actual relationships worked, and the role that language played in them. *Rob Roy* contrasts honour and credit, two words that can mean the same but have quite opposite significance.

Both Edinburgh and Washington were planned cities. Their classicism was supposed to connect back to the Greek City States and the Roman Republic. London's Westminster was a rambling old royal palace; it burned down in 1837 and was replaced by a rambling new royal palace, by Sir Charles Barry and Pugin, a Scott fan. It could almost be read like a

---

Population, Language, Market: In 1745, 5.7 million
people lived in England & Wales, 1.2 million in
Scotland and 3.0 in Ireland. Over a third of the
Scots and Irish spoke Gaelic. By 1814 England was

---

book, and being a legislature, was notably alive,
unlike Princes' Street's Scott Monument, the so-
called 'Gothic Spacerocket'.

A more recent American assault on Old England,
Martin Wiener's *British Culture and the Decline of
the Industrial Spirit* (1981) repeated the Twainite
case – Brits were too busy being gentlemen to work
– just in time for Mrs Thatcher. Such 'English
eccentrics' from this gothic environment favoured the
South in the American Civil War, among them W.E.
Gladstone, a dedicated reader of the *Waverley Novels*
along with Thomas Carlyle and John Ruskin.

But the war changed Gladstone into a democrat,
and there was a radical reading of *Ivanhoe* –
proletarian Saxons versus the 'Norman Yoke'. Victor
Hugo's *Notre Dame de Paris* (1831) took Scott's novel
up in plot and casting. Disraeli borrowed from Scott
and Carlyle and politicised *Ivanhoe* in a 'Tory Radical'
sense in *Sybil, or the Two Nations* (1845).

Scots like to talk about exporting democracy, but
they also fed North American white supremacists, in
the Orange Lodges of the Empire Loyalists of Canada
after 1783 and in the Ku Klux Klan in the 'Reconstr-
uction South'. Even 'enlightened Scotland' tolerated

10.5 million, Scotland 1.6, USA 8.0. By the Civil
War, the USA at 30 million in 1864 was about to
overtake the UK on 31 million. Literature in English
was on a roll!

a deeply undemocratic 'managed' society which for
half Scott's own life (until 1800) even allowed slavery
– among colliers and saltworkers – among its own
people.

And piracy could also be literary. As important
British publishers, Scots tended to regard non-
copyright American cheap editions as robbery.
Further, the Scots nobility, whom Scott venerated,
could also be regarded as outlaws. The great Border
abbeys were looted by local and royal 'Commend-
ators' before the post-Flodden English. Emmanuel
Todd's 'Celtic-authoritarian families' needed the 'new
economics' created by 'bare ruined choirs'.

In the red by £ 116,000
– or over £ 10 million in our money.
'My own right hand shall pay my debt' . . . but in Scots
banknotes, not gold!

15. The Uses of History

THE SCOTS applied ingenuity to history, talking up its primitiveness and pious simplicity. Was their country south of Selkirk more wild and unformed than it need have been? When Scott, Hogg and Leyden raided Liddesdale to record ballads, they said theirs was the first wheeled vehicle to be seen there, though the post-1745 maps show roads.

Even the Roman Tacitus had found the Caledonii using chariots in 43AD at Mons Graupius. Wanlock-head, a remote village in the lead-mining south, had one of the country's first libraries. The age's greatest engineer, Thomas Telford, came from Westerkirk in the 'wilds'.

As Scott observed in other writings, the Border type of social organisation wasn't just a remnant of earlier forms of society in which blood-relations counted for more than finance. Common interests meant that even enemies who were at the same stage of development counted as related. In Anglo-Scottish battles up to 1707 there was little trust in the folk of

> The Scots gentry could easily, in a small society
> surviving in the gaps between great powers, be cut
> down by injury or sheer bad luck.

the 'debateable land', governed by 'Border laws'.

These were the 'wild men' criticised by the Glasgow Archbishop Gavin Dunbar in his Cursing of Carlisle in 1520. Yet Gavin Douglas, from another Border clan and Dean of St Giles, Edinburgh, would on the eve of Flodden, 1513, finish his translation, *Eneados*, of Virgil's *Aeneid*: its first into an English tongue. He placed at its head the line: 'Of brownyis and bogillis fule is this buke.' Burns used this as the header for 'Tam O' Shanter'.

The 'wild Annandale grapeshot' of Thomas Carlyle's *Heroes and Hero-worship* (1841) was a complex chorus of language, learning, entertainment and law in somewhere that could call itself 'a hotbed of genius'. The Langholm Library Hugh MacDiarmid lived in as a boy in the 1900s was endowed by Telford (1757- 1834) and celebrated William Mickle (1735- 88) the translator of Camoens' *Lusiad*, the epic of Portuguese exploration. Was it surprising for the 'muckle toun' to welcome as its son in 1972, Neil Armstrong, the first man on the moon?

Rather than expressing landlord complacency, the Scots gentry lived 'on the margin': they raised cash as mercenaries, or in foreign service; they often switched sides, like Scott's Captain, Dugald Dalgety

Up to half of all emigrants came back to Scotland (if they
survived) but many in the pre-Imperial period stayed on
in Europe as merchants, soldiers or engineers.

in *A Legend of Montrose*. They could easily, in a small
society surviving in the gaps between great powers,
be cut down by injury or sheer bad luck.

Mark Twain wanted to condemn militarism and
picked on Scott. But there's an outlaw element in
Ivanhoe – involving Robin Hood himself – where Tom
Sawyer or Huck Finn would have felt at home. In
Rob Roy, Scott gives the Glasgow Bailie (Magistrate)
Nicol Jarvie many of the opinions that Twain would
later express, voiced effectively and subtly in the
speech of the people:

> 'But I maun hear naething about honour – we
> ken naethin here but about credit. Honour is
> a homicide and a bloodspiller that gangs
> about making frays in the street; but Credit is
> a decent honest man, that sits at hame and
> makes the pat play.'

Adam Ferguson in his *History of Civil Society*
(1767) contributed Scott's 'conjectural history':
meaning that if you didn't have full information about
a society, then social evolution suggested that if it
behaved in ways A and B, C and D would follow.
This was called the 'stadial' sequence of development,
from (1) hunter-gatherer to (2) pastoralist to (3)
farmer and to (4) merchant.

Scotland was complex enough for these stages to be found together in its various regions. The travelling tinkers came from the first inhabitants, often called 'the Egyptians' (reflecting the Scots' origin-myths). The ballads didn't die out because, being illiterate, they memorised them. Fishermen were 'marine pastoralists' just as breeders and drovers of cattle and sheep were Scottish 'agribusiness'. Then 'improvement' led to industrialised foodstuffs, raising grain-based crops to feed Europe's fastest-growing urban population, but at the cost of the animal-based diet the Scots had earlier enjoyed.

Such societies co-existed and influenced one another. Hunter-gatherers became fruit-pickers and fisherfolk; pastoralists changed from armed reivers to 'gentlemen drovers' of the *Rob Roy* sort, in the difficult time between the 1707 Union and 1745. Farmers grew flax for linen as proto-industrialists, selling it to clothe slaves on tobacco or sugar plantations. Much Atlantic produce got into the Union economy by smuggling, which features in *Redgaunt-let*; skilled men were not supposed to leave the country, but did.

16. 'This is the West, sir. When the legend becomes fact, print the legend.'

D ID SCOTT HIMSELF find a parallel across the Atlantic as Americans rapidly moved west after 1814? Settlement began with 'hunter-gatherers' – trappers or prospectors – living on Indian terms, then cattle-ranching and cowboys, then farming and then urban merchant life.

Scott's teacher, old Adam Ferguson, (1723–1816) was from Logierait on the Highland Line, pretty much where Tully-Veolan was supposed to be. He spoke Gaelic but shared Bradwardine's veneration for Livy, the great historian of Republican Rome. Both Ferguson and Livy were what were called 'Machiavellians', who believed in the links between civic morality, careful boundaries, and the right of the population to bear arms. What was feared was concentrated economic and military power.

The History Man
'Men make their own history, but they do not make it
under circumstances chosen by themselves, but . . . given
and transmitted from the past. The tradition of all the
dead generations weighs like a nightmare on the brain of
the living.' Karl Marx read Scott to the little Marxes,
reminding them they were from
Clan Campbell by descent.

Ironically such concentrated economic power came through the new technology of the American south – cotton gins, warehouses, banks, steamships, slaves.

Scott-in-America foreshadowed Frederick Jackson Turner's famous thesis of 1896 that American values were moulded on the frontier: he was not a feudal conservative but someone who saw gains through adapting, not ill-treating potential allies. Scott's novels endorsed the qualities of 'the man on the spot' and rejected interference by ideology or political or religious dogmatism. Many heroes of westward expansion were of Scots or Scots-Irish background – Sam Houston, Andrew Jackson, Jim Bowie, Davy Crockett – and episodes like the Texan wars of the 1830s emphasised this.

In *Waverley*, Highlanders are referred to as 'moving like Indians'. In this the novel anticipates the problem of learning from, and adapting to, those 'on the margin'.

Against this, Scott offered improved infrastructure: the lighthouses and turnpikes, the fancy finance of the Scottish banks, and the textile industrialist Robert Owen running a new paternalism. But, with the banks and the Scottish Highlands in trouble,

Abbotsford debt-ridden, a more pessimistic tone chokes this.

Scott identifies more with the defeated Highlanders than the booming Lowlands. He also anticipates a Victorian reaction, not of optimism but of entropy, winding-down, death. This led to much of the powerful social criticism of writers he influenced, like Carlyle, Disraeli, Ruskin and Patrick Geddes. Even Scotland's mid-Victorian excellence in the physical sciences – led by Lord Kelvin, James Clerk Maxwell – feared the 'struggle for existence' as something that weakened.

Was this a sense that the people's 'manifest destiny' must be more than national? That the community must also be pursued abroad – in the age of Burns's, Scott's, Hogg's heritors: Walt Whitman, Thomas Carlyle, John Muir, R.L. Stevenson and Patrick Geddes – following on those 'transatlantic' Scots Thomas Campbell, and John Galt?

17. An Age of Scott?

IN 1844 the Scott Monument went up in Edinburgh – Sir Walter and his dog Maida in marble, crowned by George Meikle Kemp's 200 foot Gothic spire and viewing platform inspired by the late Gothic of Melrose Abbey and Roslin Chapel. It has 64 statues from his novels and Scottish history. From up its staircase, visitors can view the capital, lowland, highland and sea. In its literal shadow lies Waverley Station (built 1845, named 1854): Scotland's link to Britain and its empire.

Monument and station symbolised Sir Walter's impact, which was civic as much as literary: the country's past – from its remotest origins to the industrial revolution – edited by one man and presented on its own doorstep. Between 1814 and 1830 if any single person represented Scotland, it was Walter Scott.

Scott was progressive, in adopting the economics of Adam Smith and the Greenock-born inventor James Watt: technical progress, within the container

Clan Scott: his reputation, despite the tourism, did lapse a bit. the centenary of 1871 was an anticlimax. Turgenev was one of the few 'greats' to attend, and no-one knew who 'Mr Turkeynuff' was.

of Scotland's Union with England. Abbotsford was the first gas-lit house in Scotland; he wanted it connected by rail to Glasgow, Edinburgh and Berwick. He pioneered publishing as a high-volume, low-cost business. After 1826 his economic ideas in *The Letters of Malachi Malagrowther* envisaged 'steering' the Scots economy through its own monetary policy.

Compared with the revolutionary Robert Burns, Scott was politically conservative, assenting to authoritarian rule by constitutional monarchy (which he partly rescued by organising King George IV's visit to Edinburgh in 1822). His politics were those of landowners, lawyers, ministers, bailies, business-men; though aware of social problems. This projected itself by imaginatively creating an accessible culture, at all levels. His most engaging figures are 'ordinary' Scots.

On behalf of this cultural aim, he used new methods of organisation and communication: science and economics applied to land; the extension of law into commerce and social relations; the reconstruc-tion of towns; the expansion of foreign trade. And from all of these he created human, *humane* examples.

Things recovered with Stevenson (see *Kidnapped* (1886) and *The Master of Ballantrae* (1889), good studies by Andrew Long (1906) and John Buchan's impressive single volume *Life* of 1932.

In this he acted as an adaptor and populariser of Scots advances in the infant social sciences. His art embraced translation, drama, folklore research, journalism, scholarly editing, history, geography, narrative romance, historical novels, illustration, contemporary history, and the sort of commentary in his *Journal*, that we would now call a blog.

To do all this he created different voices: Walter Scott, 'The Author of *Waverley*', those of his contemporaries and of his own characters – not limited to those he agreed with. In the difficult end-phase of his career he addressed his audience direct.

There was a direct literary legacy. It's impossible to think of Robert Louis Stevenson or Neil Munro, John Buchan or Neil Gunn without reference back to Scott. Even the 'bad side' of Scots literature, the too-marketable kailyard or the sensationalism of 'tartan noir' has roots traceable to him. Among contemporary writers his influence in various ways shows itself on James Robertson, Allan Massie or Alasdair Gray. But its magnitude is also historical and political.

Scott could achieve this in a country that had earlier been a field of European combat. It was

expanding abroad, in contact with different stages of social evolution, and involving his countryfolk at all levels. In this sense he was far more than a writer. Like him or hate him, he was a multitalented political fact.

Scott's last great project *Life of Napoleon* was a biography of a man, as a Corsican an outsider to France, who defined his new nation and changed Europe by leadership, science and war. In 1799, his Army of Egypt discovered the Rosetta stone, the great decoder of the ancient world. Scott could, and did, reflect that his own name and his folk studies (generously defined) had a similar – though cultural – currency in Scotland and Britain, though ultimately his loyalty was both supranational, and Scots:

> Breathes there the man with soul so dead
> That never to himself hath said
> This is my own, my native land!

Appendices

(1) SIR WALTER SCOTT'S CV

Name: Sir Walter Scott, Baronet (1819)

Address: born College Wynd, Edinburgh, lived in George Square and Castle Street, Edinburgh, 1771-1826; also at Sandyknowe, Bath and Kelso; second homes: Lasswade Cottage, Midlothian 1798-1804; Ashiestiel 1804-11 and Abbotsford 1811-31.

Family: 1797 married Charlotte Carpenter (1770-1826), children Sophia (b.1799), Walter (b.1801), Anne (b.1803) and Charles (b.1805).

Education: English, Latin, Italian, French, Spanish, German, acquired at the Edinburgh High School and Kelso, 1779-83, and law at the University of Edinburgh, 1783-5.

Employment History:
1792-1799 Law: apprenticeship 1785-1788, then advocate; Sheriff-Depute of Selkirk, 1799-

1832; Clerk to the Court of Session, 1806-32; Advocates' Librarian, throughout career.

1800-1803 Collecting with James Hogg and John Leyden the oral ballads of the Scottish Borderers, published as *the Minstrelsy of the Scottish Border* in 1802. Editing historical and literary texts, mainly seventeenth century, notably Dryden and Swift.

1804-1814 Writing a series of book-length narrative poems, from *The Lay of the Last Minstrel* to *Marmion* and *The Lady of the Lake*, mainly based on Scottish history in the medieval-renaissance period.

1814-1831 The *Waverley Novels*, starting with that title, in *historical* order as follows:

- *The Fortunes of Nigel* (1822) – The reign of James I
- *A Legend of Montrose* (1819) – The Civil War in Scotland
- *Old Mortality* (1816) – The 'Covenanting war' of the 1670s
- *The Bride of Lammermoor* (1819) – Family feuds in the time of the Union, 1707
- *Rob Roy* (1817) – Financial intrigue, cattle raiding clans in 1720s

- *The Heart of Midlothian* (1818) – The Porteous Riots and consequences, 1736
- *Waverley* (1814) – 1745-6 Jacobite rebellion
- *Guy Mannering* (1815) – South-West Scotland, inheritance intrigue, 1760s
- *Redgauntlet* (1824) – Frustrated Jacobite plot in the 1760s
- *The Chronicles of the Canongate* (1827) – Contemporary Scotland in the 1820s

For a full list of all Scott's works, including fiction, prose and poetry, visit The Walter Scott Digital Archive (University of Edinburgh) *www.walterscott.lib.ed.ac.uk/works/index.html* or *www.clanscotland.org.uk*

Other Interests: Fishing, riding, military exercises, dogs, eating and drinking, collecting historical curiosities, commerce.

Referees: the Rt. Hon. Charles William Henry Montagu Douglas-Scott, His Grace the Duke of Buccleuch, Bowhill;
Henry Dundas, Viscount Melville, Arniston;
Professor Adam Ferguson of Raith, Fife.

Contemporaries, Like:
Madame de Stael, 1766-1817

Robert Stevenson, engineer, 1772-1850
George Stephenson, engineer, 1772-1850
Horace Walpole, aesthete, 1717-1797
Arthur, Duke of Wellington, 1769-1852
J.M.W. Turner, painter, 1775-1851
William Wilberforce, opponent of slavery, 1759-1833
William Wordsworth, poet, 1770-1850

Contemporaries, Dislike:
Jeremy Bentham, utilitarian reformer, 1748-1832
Napoleon Bonaparte, Emperor, 1769-1820
Lord Brougham, Whig reformer, 1778-1868
William Cobbett, journalist, 1763-1835
Thomas Jefferson, US President, 1743-1826
John Martin, painter, 1789-1854
James Mill, philosopher, 1773-1836

(2) BOOKS ON SCOTT AND SCOTLAND

Sir Walter Scott:

John Gibson Lockhart, *Memoirs of the Life of Sir Walter Scott*, Bart. (7 volumes), Edinburgh, 1837-8

John Buchan, *Sir Walter Scott*, London: Cassell, 1932

Edwin Muir, *Scott and Scotland*, London: 1936

Edgar Johnson, *Sir Walter Scott*, (2 volumes), London, 1970

David Daiches, *Walter Scott and his World*, London: Thames and Hudson, 1971

Jerome Mitchell, *The Walter Scott Operas*, University of Alabama, 1975

Alan Bold, ed., *The Long-Forgotten Melody*, New York: Vision, 1981

Douglas Gifford, ed., *The History of Scottish Literature* (Volume 3: Nineteenth Century), Aberdeen University Press, 1988

Allan Massie, *The Ragged Lion*, Sceptre, 1994

John Sutherland, *The Life of Walter Scott: A Critical Biography*, Oxford University Press, 1995

Iain Gordon Brown, ed., *Abbotsford and Sir Walter Scott*, Edinburgh: RCAHMS, 2003.

Caroline McCracken-Flesher, *Possible Scotlands: Walter Scott and the Story of Tomorrow*, Oxford University Press, 2005

Stuart Kelly, *Scott-land: The Man Who Invented a Nation*, Edinburgh: Birlinn, 2011

Fiona Robertson, ed., *The Edinburgh Companion to Sir Walter Scott*, Edinburgh University Press, 2012

Background:

W.F. Gray, ed., Lord Cockburn's Memorials of his Time, 1854, Edinburgh: Grant, 1945

T.C. Smout, *A History of the Scottish People*, Glasgow: Collins, 1968

Christopher Harvie, *Scotland and Nationalism*, London: Allen and Unwin, 1977-2004

Martin Wiener, *British Culture and the Decline of*

the Industrial Spirit, Cambridge University Press, 1981

Ted Cowan, ed., *The People's Past: Scottish Folk, Scottish History*, Edinburgh: Polygon, 1991

Kitty Cruft, *John Dunbar and Richard Fawcett, The Buildings of Scotland: Borders*, New Haven and London: Yale University Press, 2006

Christopher Harvie, *Scotland the Brief: A Short History of a Nation* (new edition), Argyll Publishing, 2013

Christopher Fleet, Margaret Wilkes and Charles W J Withers, *Scotland: Mapping the Nation*, Edinburgh: Birlinn, 2012

(3) SCOTT AND SCOTLAND ONLINE

- The National Library of Scotland
  www.nls.uk

- The National Portrait Gallery
  www.npg.org.uk

- The Scottish National Portrait Gallery
  www.nationalgalleries.org/portraitgallery

- The National Trust for Scotland
  www.nts.org.uk/Home

- The Prestonpans Tapestry
  www.prestonpanstapestry.org/tapestry

- The Edinburgh Sir Walter Scott Club
  www.eswsc.com

- The Dictionary of National Biography
  www.oup.com/oxforddnb/info/subscribe

- Traquair House: History
  www.traquair.co.uk/brief-history-traquair-and-family

- Illustrating Scott: A Database of Printed Illustrations to the Waverley Novels, 1814-1901 *illustratingscott.lib.ed.ac.uk*

- SCRAN *www.scran.ac.uk*

- Scott Monument Virtual Tour *sites.scran.ac.uk/scottmon*

- Abbotsford House (The Home of Sir Walter Scott) *www.scottsabbotsford.co.uk/*

Index

Index

Index